Sip It, Dip It, Lap It

C000058806

Written by Monica Hughes
Photographs by Steve Lumb

Collins

Sip it, Sam.

Sam sips it.

Dip it in, Sid.

Sid dips it in.

Dad sips it.

Pam dips it in.

Nan taps it.

Tim dips it in.

Dad taps it.

Pat dips it in.

Dip it in, Mat.

Mat dips it in.

Sip it.

Dip it.

 Ideas for reading

Written by Clare Dowdall, PhD
Lecturer and Primary Literacy Consultant

Learning objectives: hear and say sounds in the order in which they occur; read simple words by sounding out and blending the phonemes all through the word from left to right; read a range of familiar and common words and simple sentences independently; extend their vocabulary, exploring the meaning and sounds of new words; use phonic knowledge to write simple regular words and make phonetically plausible attempts at more complex words

Curriculum links: Knowledge and Understanding of the World: Find out about, and identify, some features of living things, objects and events they observe

Focus phonemes: s, a, t, p, i, n, d, m

Word count: 43

Getting started

- Write the words *sip, dip, tap,* on the whiteboard. Ask children to blend the sounds in each word to read them.

- Using magnetic letters for the focus phonemes: *s a t p i n d m,* ask the children to make as many three-letter words as they can with a partner.

- Practise reading the words that the children have made, modelling how to blend phonemes to read each word.

- Hand out the books. Read the title together and check that children understand the vocabulary. Ask the children to describe what is happening in the picture.

Reading and responding

- Ask children to read the book from the beginning to the end independently, pointing to each word as they read.

- Listen to each child as you move around the group and support their attempts to blend and read fluently.

- Stop the children and ask them to focus on particular pages and describe what is happening to a partner.